From the
Pit
to the
Palace

Dr. Gail James

Strive International Publishing Group is a division of Courageous Media Group. For more information on the authors, ordering, book signings, or to sponsor an event, contact us at: info@courageouswomanmag.com.

Edited/formatted by Shonell Bacon
Publisher/Book Coach – Telishia Berry

ISBN: 978-1-7378761-0-6

Want more info about publishing? Contact Telishia at info@courageouswomanmag.com and www.courageouswomanmag.com.

Dedication

This book is dedicated to my mother Annie Mae Fuse; my father Gaston George Bedminster; my husband Rick James Jr.; my daughter Abigail Jarvis; and my three sons, Kelvin Samuel II, Khristjan Samuel, and Tyrell James.

Acknowledgments

I would like to acknowledge My Lord and Savior Jesus Christ, for it was and still is his Grace and Mercy that brought me through it all.

I would also like to acknowledge Ms. Lucina Jarvis for nurturing me, Minister Tangie Bradley for being my right hand throughout this process, and Telishia Berry for her assistance and push to allow me to bring this vision to life.

Table of Contents

Life Begins

Gail James is my name, and a survivor is who I am. I was born on the amazing Caribbean Island of St. Thomas, U.S. Virgin Islands. I was born to a mother with ten children and a father who had 15 children prior to my birth. My mother would eventually have twelve children, of which three daughters belonged to my father. My father was a rolling stone. He fathered two additional daughters while married to my mother. Their births were between my baby sister's birth and my birth. My life was not comfortable living in a house with five sisters and four brothers. My sisters and I lived in the upstairs section of our home, while my four brothers lived downstairs.

Living with my siblings was difficult, to say the least. My siblings found it convenient to blame me for my father's negative behavior. For reasons unknown, I was considered the black sheep of the family. Everything that went wrong in my siblings' lives would somehow become my fault. They tormented me constantly, and my life was extremely sad, compounded with difficulties. From the age of seven until I was eleven, three of my brothers molested me frequently. This began a tumultuous life of devastation, filled with hurt, pain, anger, and rejection. It was a dismal reality that felt like a downward spiral with no end to it in sight.

One day, while attending my elementary school in the Virgin Islands, there was excessive blood all over my skirt. My teacher saw it and took me to the nurse's office to find out why I was bleeding. After 45 minutes of questioning by the nurse, I finally told her that one of my brothers had sexually abused me the day before. Shortly afterward, the police were called, and three unmarked detective cars arrived with sirens blazing. The detectives came into the nurse's office and began to ask questions. After speaking with the nurses, they called my mother to the school. My mother arrived, stood at the nurse's office door, and looked at me with utter disgust as though I had done something wrong. After hearing why she was called to the school, my mother and I left to go home. My mother called one of my older brothers to mediate the pending situation. My elder brother asked the 21-year-old brother if he had sexually abused me. He repeatedly denied any knowledge of it and insisted he had no idea what I was saying. Finally, he admitted to the sexual abuse, and my mother looked at me and said, "You good-for-nothing dog, you. You knew what you were doing, and you wanted it."

I nearly evaporated through the floor. I was expecting a hug, baby, I'm sorry, or I love you. Unfortunately, I did not receive any expressions of remorse or compassion from the one who was supposed to protect me. All I received from my mother was accusation after accusation that it was my fault. I do not understand why I even expected more. I am the black sheep of the family.

At an early age, I learned that someone else's opinion of me does not have to become my reality.

> **"**
>
> Many things are worse than defeat, and compromising with evil is one of them.

Obstacles

After my brother's confession, I endured more physical, mental, verbal, and emotional abuse. The Department of Human Services gave my mother strict rules and guidelines to follow because my brother and I lived in the same house. My mother decided there was no reason to protect me, seeing I was the problem. In her mind, I created this mess; now, I had to deal with it. She felt this could have been prevented if I'd kept the family secret. Too often, we hear, "What happens in this house stays in this house." This leads to buried secrets of manipulation, mental trauma, and unfathomable pain for years and sometimes a lifetime.

My mother could not see how her thinking was negatively impacting not only my brother's freedom but also her freedom. The Department of Human Services arrived at our house one day in a 15-passenger white van. They told my mother, "Since you won't protect your minor child, and it seems you're too busy protecting your adult son, we will protect her by removing her from this house immediately."

That same day, I was removed from my home and taken to a group home for girls who were behaving badly. This was notably the only juvenile home in the Virgins Islands. I had done nothing wrong to deserve to be here. The Department of Human Services said they would protect me because my mother would not, and they were doing a poor job at it, too. All I wanted was for my mother and siblings to love me enough to protect me. Now I found myself in a place exposed to the same inappropriate sexual behaviors I wanted to escape. I was assigned to a bedroom shared by another young lady. At nighttime, she would sneak boys into the room through the window to have sex while she lay beside me. They were close enough to rub their elbows against me. Why was this happening to me, and how could I escape?

I decided this was not the way I wanted to live, so I ran away to the home of a married couple I used to babysit for. They told me they could not let me stay because they would get in trouble because I was a minor. So, they called Human Services, and they took me back into the group home, where the conditions had not improved. In fact, the conditions were severely worse.

After I had been there a while, my father had a landscaping job for two of the most prominent judges in the Virgin Islands. They saw my name come across their desk and asked why I had to be removed from my home. They knew my father had a reputation for assaulting people. He did not know how to control his temper. So, the judges instructed three Marshals to bring my father into custody to prevent him from killing his stepson, who molested me.

When the Marshals finally found my dad, he had already sharpened two machetes and was sharpening the third one. They took my father into custody and were told by the judge that he would be kept for three days so that he could calm down and not get into trouble. The judges promised him they would deal with the case appropriately. My father was let go after three days, and he waited day after day to hear if his stepson had been charged with molestation of a minor.

Eventually, my father went to the judge and asked about the status of the case and how much longer it would take for a court date. The judge responded to him by saying, "You don't know?"

"Know what?" my father asked.

To his surprise, the judge told him my mother and his stepson had already negotiated the case. He was sentenced to probation and community service and would be registered as a sex offender for the rest of his life.

Upon finding out this shocking and disturbing news, my father was irate. He went home and violently slammed my mother's face into the kitchen door, breaking her nose and jaw. It's not a surprise that my mother and father eventually separated and went their own way.

Mistakes are a great educator when one is honest enough to admit them and willing to learn from them.

Trauma

All trauma can have real, lasting effects; it doesn't matter if that trauma is connected to relationships, work, finances, etc. Many people experience physical ailments such as memory loss, sleep deprivation, and suicidal thoughts. Trauma can also be manifested in psychological, mental, and emotional ways. It can affect the human body in so many ways that others do not realize its impact—until it's too late.

For anyone who has experienced trauma, the memory recall from these violent experiences will remain unless professional help is received. We must realize that we are not designed to manage the weight of rape and molestation after being abused and used on our own. We need help to break free from our past and must not be afraid to ask for it or receive it when it comes.

Trauma from past relationships and even our childhood threatens to hold us hostage and restrict us from being free indeed. It can delimit us as we build walls to protect us, and then we become prisoners of our thoughts. Our lives are not fulfilled, and we need to walk out our purpose. This can cause us to behave in a way that is not particularly in line with who we are. We can react disproportionately to the context of a situation because we are not operating in logic but in fear. Our behaviors can be passive-aggressive by responding in pessimistic and unproductive ways. We can become toxic, spewing venom and not even realizing it is happening until we are made aware of it.

> Every tomorrow has two handles. We can take hold of it by the handle of anxiety or by the handle of faith.

Stumbling Blocks

Throughout my life, I've had to live in multiple homes. God has always touched the hearts of individuals to open their doors to me. They were compassionate and had empathy for me because of the situations I was faced with. At the time, I had no support or prior guidance when I needed it the most. I returned home due to a lack of stable housing, but this reunion would not last long. At 14, my mother broke my arm after I arrived home late from my part-time after-school job. Sadly, she never considered that I did not have transportation to and from work. I walked most of the way and would occasionally be blessed with a ride. My mother used any excuse possible to beat me violently. It became so easy for her to beat me with a broomstick and break my arm without a second thought. When she finally stopped hitting me, one of my brothers asked her if he could take me to the hospital because it looked like my arm was broken. Mother told him, "No, don't touch my car before I break your arm, too." There were no words for the callous and acrimonious behavior shown toward me.

I tried to find time to go to the hospital but had to wait until everyone was asleep. Around 10 p.m., I packed some clothes in a black garbage bag. I climbed out the window with the bag of clothes, looking back to ensure the coast was clear. The last thing I needed was to get caught going out the window after she had already broken my right arm. I did not need to have both arms out of commission. I placed the bag in the trunk of an old BMW parked on the road. The trunk never closed, so I left the clothes and went to the hospital. When I finally arrived at the hospital, the physician refused to touch my broken arm because I was a minor.

Their response extremely saddened me, so I went to find an adult with whom I was familiar. He frequently came to my mother's business to purchase items. I thought to myself, maybe he could help me. I looked for him to see if he could and was willing to help me. After finding him, he happily agreed to help. I told him I needed him to sign his name authorizing the hospital to provide the care I needed for my broken arm. He was 19 years old, and I was 14 at the time. He drove me to the hospital and signed the paperwork for me. He was such an amazing, kind, caring, and compassionate person.

The relationship with him eventually became more than friends. He helped me in every area of my life possible. He assisted in buying my school supplies, uniforms, giving me money for lunch, and transporting me to and from school and work. He became my safe place.

> You have got to have hope. Without hope, life is meaningless.

Real Effects

Depression and anxiety are common effects of trauma. Many people live their lives in a perpetually sad, low-spirited state. Sometimes, a person's behavior does not make sense when they are battling depression. One's behavior can be in total contrast to who one really is because of the subtle and undetected changes occurring because of this illness.

I remember being depressed and suffering from anxiety. I secluded myself and refused to interact with friends or family members, especially those who would ask questions. I constantly pushed people away, and I isolated myself. I was ashamed of my situation and felt completely overwhelmed. The answers to change my problem seemed so simple yet complex at the same time.

It's not unusual for someone in an overwhelming situation beyond their control to experience depression or anxiety. Wide-ranging thoughts come in like a flood with no warning or notice. Emotions are like a rollercoaster and a teeter-totter constantly going up and down. One can feel happy and optimistic one moment and in tears within seconds.

As for me, I can remember feeling like I did not deserve to have anything good in my life. I did not feel attractive, intelligent, or worthy. The inconceivable trauma I endured, I wish this on no one. It strips away your essence and sometimes leaves you unrecognizable to yourself or others. Looking in the mirror, you are left to try and figure out whose image is glaring back at you.

When battling with out-of-control emotions and trying to figure out who you really are, a spirit of self-sabotage can manifest and add to the mix. When a person is depressed, sadly, this becomes their small world. They begin feeling worthless and anticipate terrible things will happen to them. The mind plays all sorts of tricks on them, telling lies that they are unloved and will be abandoned by anyone close to them. This stronghold gains power when left unchecked and untreated, allowing the victims to create situations to support their narrative.

Examples of this are:

- Repeatedly ending relationships for no reason before the other person leaves them

- Having desires to achieve specific goals but not taking the time to prepare or make any movement to accomplish them adequately
- Overcomplicating simple processes and solutions, which makes it harder to accomplish and complete the tasks and succeed
- Continually engaging in situations and relationships that are not logical, sound, or beneficial, only convenient
- Approaching situations based on emotions and considering them to be authentic and valid because of how they feel versus what is occurring

I'll be ok. Just not today.

When Good Is Not Good

He treated me like a queen for two years until he learned that I was abandoned by my family and considered an outcast. It was noticeable that his mindset had changed, and I knew this because his behavior and care for me were different. I went from being the most important person in his life to being the most irrelevant. I was no longer a priority; I became optional. I felt this way because he showed me through his words and actions toward me.

He began to beat me daily, from kicking me with steel-toe boots in my ribs to punching and slapping me in the face. He beat me violently weekly because I confronted him about his cheating and lying. By this time, I wanted out of the relationship. The physical abuse increased, and so did his infidelity. Both became too much for me to bear. I had no choice but to place restraining orders against him. I would even complain to the police, but it did not matter. As a result of the restraining orders, I had to find my own apartment if I was going to survive.

God blessed me with an efficient apartment for $250 a month. However, this forced me to have to work two jobs after school just to be able to pay my rent. Though being in my own apartment brought me peace of mind, it also carried significant difficulties when trying to go to school and work. My school and one of my jobs were located on the opposite side of the island. His mother, who loved me like her child, cared enough to give me her car and purchase another for herself. I could still see God at work in what seemed the worst. We agreed that I would pay her $40 a month for the car to teach me responsibilities.

For once in my life, things were coming together. I had two jobs, an apartment, and a car. I finally felt like I was good, and things were looking up. Unfortunately, he was not willing to give up on the relationship. After all the abuse he inflicted upon me, he continued to stalk and harass me. He went as far as kidnapping me and taking me to his home. He held me hostage for an entire week. During the time I was his hostage, he would threaten me with a 12-gauge and 9-mm gun constantly. Sometimes, I thought I would never be rescued from his violent clutches, but God stepped in when I needed Him most.

My absolute best friend, who had not seen me in school for nearly a week, contacted my sister. She told her that she thought something might have happened to me because it was not like me to miss school. My friend directed them to his house while talking to my sister, telling her she believed I was being held against my will. Because of my best friend's genuine care and concern, my mother, father, and sister came to his house to rescue me. He opened the door and began talking to my father. My father did not show up to ask questions. Dad was armed with a machete, my sister had a bat, and my mother had an empty brandy bottle.

My family started calling for me to come upstairs, but they had no idea I was being held at gunpoint. My father became furious and started yelling and ordering me to come upstairs. Although I feared my ex and the two guns pointing at me, I was more fearful of my father. I decided to make a run for it. As I ran frantically to my dad, surprisingly, my ex-boyfriend did not shoot me in the back. He slammed the door behind me, and I continued to run toward my family.

Sometimes, the most powerful thing you can say is nothing at all.

How Did I Get Here?

There are moments in your life that seem so surreal. It feels as though you are having an out-of-body experience. Your senses become heightened, and everything is viewed in slow motion. You notice and remember the most minuscule details.

That is how I felt during some of the scariest moments of my life. At one particular moment, my ex-boyfriend blocked my cousin's car with his van, jumped out of the van, and raced to the passenger-side door. I barely had time to scream before he pulled and dragged me through the window.

After throwing me into his van, he took me to the beach and began hitting me repeatedly in the back of my head with his 9mm. Due to the forceful blows I encountered, I was knocked unconscious. I am grateful to God that an onlooker saw it and called the police. When the police arrived on the scene, he walked around me with the gun in his hand, saying that he would kill me and then kill himself. While I was lying barely conscious in the sand, the police were able to disarm him without incident.

I asked myself, "How could this be happening to me?" I wanted to have at least one good day. I could not envision what transpired on that day by any stretch of my imagination. Less than three hours prior, I woke up in good spirits, excited and anticipating a great day. Now, I was facing a 9mm gun after being kidnapped again.

So many thoughts were running through my mind. Is this how my story will end? Is this man who once loved me going to kill me? Will he torture me by burying me alive? All these thoughts flooding my mind seemed like valid, strong possibilities. He had already shown me his proclivities and love for abuse and violence. The only question in my mind was, "How far will he go this time?"

All I could do as he pulled my hair, cursed at me, and called me names was think about all the times he abused me. He would punch me in the face until it was bloody and swollen. How could someone who was once so caring and loving be so violent and cold in his behavior toward me?

After he had finished beating me, he would tell me to get out of his face and clean myself up.

Apparently, he felt that it was my fault, and I brought this on myself. I inconvenienced him by being there, forcing him to take time out of his day to beat me down.

By the arrogant smirk on his face, he functioned as though I should've thanked him for the mercy extended to me. I know it could have been worse, and in his mind, he should have given me what I truly deserved, whatever he considered that to be.

I really do not know how it got to that point. I remember thinking in the moments like: "How did I allow myself to accept such treatment from a man who is supposed to love me? Am I less than a dog? I would be better off dead!" The last thought hit the hardest and echoed in my mind repeatedly. There was much uncertainty in my life, but one thing was certain; if I were close to him, he would beat me again. After he was exhausted enough to stop, I would lie wherever he left me, dazed and desiring to fade away into unconsciousness to escape the pain and misery.

Finally, there came a day when I grew tired of the beatings and constant abuse. The abuse was not only physical but mental and emotional. I decided to take control of my life because I refused to continue giving that control to someone else. I said to myself, "I'm not going to allow this to continue!" I convinced myself that I was determined not to run away. Instead, I would take my own life. It would be on my terms, not his.

I remember him beating me so badly in his house that I cried hysterically as I went into the bathroom and swallowed a whole bottle of Tylenol. The Tylenol caused me to vomit violently until my throat and stomach hurt and burned from the acid. It didn't have the impact I had hoped, so I stood, looking at myself in the mirror and repeatedly asking, "Why me?" I could not seem to make it all stop.

I stayed in the bathroom, sitting quietly and thinking that life couldn't get much worse than it was. I looked under the sink and saw a bottle of Clorox bleach and thought this would surely end all my problems. I opened the bottle of bleach and began to drink it, hoping to die from it. But I did not. I thought surely this would be my last time being beaten, and he would later find me and feel sorry for how badly he had treated me. However, despite the part of me that wanted to die, there was a more significant part that wanted to live!

> Sometimes, you need to step outside, get some air, and remind yourself of who you are and where you want to be.

Hindsight

Looking back, I know deep down inside that I did not want to die. I was so tired of the constant beating and unrelenting anger unleashed upon me. As bad as things were, I could not imagine how our relationship would finally end. I had endured being kidnapped at gunpoint, held hostage, and threatened to be killed. But I survived!

I never imagined or believed these things would ever happen to me in a million lifetimes. You hear about them or see them played out on television and think, "That is weird! This cannot be real life! That's a far stretch! That would never happen to a real person!"

These are thoughts of someone on the outside looking in because no one in their right mind would willingly place themselves in a situation to be abused and accept it. The logical thing to do would be to get out. I have learned, however, through my own experience, that what we call love makes us do crazy things. Who would volunteer to be abused repeatedly? This is what happens when you feel trapped and see no way out. You stay and suffer at the hands of your abuser until you reach the end of yourself and cry out for help.

You would think that after the initial incident, which was not a mistake or a provocation, I would see the handwriting on the wall and know this was a preview of the coming attraction. The first punch thrown and the occurrence of the first humiliating moment indicate where things are going in the relationship. It is common for the victims to question their self-worth while trying to figure out what they did wrong. There are no answers to justify what has happened, but the abuser will always find a way to cause you to see things through their lens.

As much as we would like to believe that abuse doesn't happen like that, it's more common than most people realize. The reason is that most abusers are not *all* bad; many of them have so much good in them. Not that I'm covering for the wrong they do or the pain they inflict, but many are fighting demons they don't know how to control.

Most abusers are only repeating what they have seen or experienced. They have the potential to be great husbands, fathers, and leaders. They must learn that cycles can be broken. At the beginning of your courtship, he loves and respects you as a woman with genuine care. These sweet words and moments are what you remember when things start going south. The way they caressed you and made you feel special, you want to believe in them. You do not want to give up on them so quickly because your heart is involved. You feel bound to them and obligated to weather the storm with them, no matter how bumpy the road is. You begin finding ways yourself things like:

"This is not the person I met."

"They're just stressed."

"When things get better in their life, they will treat me even better."

"If I could just do what they ask of me, everything would be all right. They will change how they treat me."

The truth is that those are usually all lies. We deceive ourselves about the situation. We believe that decency, love, respect, and good treatment are based on our ability to meet someone else's expectations. This should not be the case in a relationship.

Yes, we feel more invigorated about life and attending to someone else's needs when our needs are met. However, relationships should not be completely unconditional. Yes, you read that right—relationships should not be completely unconditional. That is something that I believe strongly.

> Never lower your worth for worthless people.

Unconditional Love

Unconditional love is different from being in a relationship with someone. You can love someone unconditionally, but that does not mean you must choose to be in a relationship with them. More importantly, it does not mean that you must decide to stay in an unhealthy relationship with them.

Unconditional love has the power to say, "I love you, but I will not stay in a broken relationship." Loving someone unconditionally does not mean you cannot choose yourself, especially when abused in a relationship. There is no honor or trophy for sacrificing yourself to someone mentally unstable, emotionally unavailable, or narcissistic.

Relationships, including romantic ones, should be based on healthy boundaries, mutual respect, and love. Naturally, when the normal becomes unpredictable, boundaries are crossed, mutual respect is lost, and love ceases to exist, relationships will end up suffering and eventually fade.

This is due to the reality that relationships and unconditional love are not the same!

We can love someone unconditionally without being in a relationship with them. That is not to say that every relationship does not have growing pains. This does not mean that someone will not mess up. Everyone has the potential to say or do something toxic or wrong in a relationship. There is no such thing as a perfect relationship. It is as perfect as two individuals make it.

Nevertheless, as you progress in your relationship, character flaws will appear from both sides. Matters of the heart eventually are revealed, and blinders should be removed to proceed cautiously. Understanding an individual's ability and limitations in specific areas does strengthen our will to love them for who they are. We all are flawed and need help and grace as we walk through life's journey. In doing so, we must accept the risk that comes with the vacillating emotions and the spontaneous shifts included in the package deal.

But we must also remember that if we are willing to deal with who someone really is, accepting their good intentions must be understood. All of us will mess up or fall short in areas of life. This is different from someone deliberately harming you.

Mental abuse, physical altercations, belittling, humiliating, demeaning, passive-aggressive jabs, and other actions are not shortcomings. They are toxic behaviors or traits embedded within one's soul. Abuse, violence, and mental manipulation have no place in a relationship with any hope of a future.

Sometimes, walking away has nothing to do with weakness but everything to do with strength. We walk away not because we want others to realize our worth and value but because we finally recognize our own.

Immediate Rush

I eventually grew tired of being the main woman and replaced it with my desire to be the only woman. I was worthy of it and wanted to be loved and appreciated by someone who understood I was enough. I finally loved myself enough to know I deserved more than he could give.

When I met him, he had no children. Within two years of the relationship, he impregnated two different women simultaneously. I tried repeatedly to leave this relationship, but my escape never lasted long. He always found and physically abused me because I attempted to end the relationship. I thought things would be different this time because I no longer lived in the home with him. Unfortunately, I was wrong. I thought this was the last time I would have to deal with him and his abuse. I was about to learn otherwise. After approximately six months of living in my apartment, I discovered I was pregnant with his baby.

As if that was not enough unexpected news, I found out the same two women who had children by him two years ago were both pregnant again. Upon finding out the two women were pregnant, I told him we needed to talk. He arrived at my apartment later that evening. After he arrived, I was in my apartment with three male friends braiding their hair. He showed up and began cursing and banging on the door nonstop. I instructed my friends not to open the door. However, they were so afraid that they got up, opened the door, walked out, and left me there. All I could think was that this was going to be horrible. I know how he thinks; he thinks of me as his property. I just knew this was going to end horribly. However, I still took the opportunity to tell him I was pregnant, but I wanted an abortion because we were no longer in a relationship, and I was tired of playing second fiddle.

After hearing the news, he wanted to stop me from having an abortion. He started beating me violently. My body contacted every wall in my apartment. I felt like I and my baby would die that day. What confused me was that instead of having a civilized conversation with me to convince me why I should not have an abortion, he beat me profusely. This puts his daughter's life and my life in jeopardy. After fervent praying and asking God for strength, I decided to keep my little angel and give birth to her. By this time, my only choice was to live with his mother, who nursed me back to health. I was in my last year of high school and working two after-school jobs. His mother was very supportive and ensured I completed high school and had all my needs met.

I recall feeling insignificant, abused, abandoned, and rejected. I remember giving my biological mother an invitation to my high school graduation, and she threw the invitation back at me. She told me she had better things to do with her time and not expect her to be there.

At this time, I was going into my 6-month gestation period, two weeks before my high school graduation. While in class, catching up on my schoolwork, I started feeling cramp-like aches in my stomach. The school bell rang, and it was lunchtime. I followed my friends to the stairs to the gymnasium, where we always sat during lunch. The pains in my lower abdomen got significantly worse as time went by. Before long, I stopped laughing with my friends and started balling up in a fetal position. My best friend ran to the school's office and asked someone to help me because I was in excruciating pain. The school's secretary put me in her car and drove me to the hospital. She called his mother and told her I was in labor with her grandchild. On her drive to the emergency room, she stopped by my biological mother's business to tell her that I was in labor and that she was taking me to the hospital.

On May 31, 1990, at 2:30 p.m., I gave birth to my daughter, who weighed only 2 pounds. Due to her significantly low birth weight and distress during labor, my daughter was immediately rushed to the NICU and placed in an incubator. She would remain in NICU until she gained enough weight and was healthy enough to be released and cared for at home.

After my mother closed her business for the day, she, my father, and my sister came to the hospital to visit me and see my daughter. Once arriving at the hospital, only my sister and my father came upstairs to visit me. My mother stayed in the car for two hours in the hot sun and refused to come in and see me. This was so painful. It felt like nothing I did or could ever do would be enough to earn her love. At that moment, I felt so alone, abandoned, and rejected; however, I did thank God for my daughter's paternal grandmother. Not only did she come to the hospital, but she also was the only person helping me as I was attempting to give birth for the first time in my life. Right then, I promised myself to love my daughter unconditionally, not because of, but despite all and any flaws she may have.

It had been two weeks since my precious gift from God, my baby girl, was born. I would stay with her in the hospital from sunup to sundown. She was improving, in my opinion, but what did I know? She was my first child. I often would go to my biological mother's business and sit there talking with her to take a break from watching my baby in an incubator while dealing with the fact that I could not hold her in my arms. Sitting and speaking with my biological mother was a welcoming distraction because it beat watching my daughter as she was hooked up to all these machines.

On October 1, 1990, as I sat at my mother's business with her, an ambulance came speeding with sirens blasting, and they stopped at my mother's business. The ambulance driver asked if either of us was the mother of Abigail Jarvis, and my mother asked, "What do you want?"

"If they are asking for Abigail's mother," I said to my mother, "it's because something is wrong." I at once responded, saying, "I am Abigail's mother. What's wrong?"

The ambulance driver responded, "Your daughter has stopped breathing, and we must immediately take her to Puerto Rico. You must come with us right now."

As I began to cry profusely, my mother looked at me and asked, "Why are you crying? It is better that Abigail dies than you die." I did not even respond to that comment.

The driver instructed me to get into the ambulance immediately because I needed to fly to Puerto Rico on a helicopter with my daughter. There, she would receive the proper medical care she needed to survive. My daughter and I were flown to Puerto Rico without any clothing or necessities due to my daughter's distress.

After arriving in Puerto Rico, I was determined to stay in Puerto Rico with my daughter because I did not want to leave her. I had to sleep on the chairs in the clinic area of the hospital because there was nowhere else to go. They asked me to leave the clinic because the janitor would complain about me sleeping in the clinic when he opened it each morning. I stayed in Puerto Rico with the clothing on my back, washing out my underwear daily in the hospital bathroom. Not once did my mother, father, sisters, or brothers come to check on me or my newborn daughter.

However, my daughter's paternal grandmother remained faithful, kind, and loving toward me and her granddaughter. She was the only person that cared enough to come to Puerto Rico to see how her granddaughter and I were doing. She arrived with a round-trip ticket to St. Thomas for me and demanded that I attend my high school graduation. I told her I could not leave my daughter alone, but she insisted I return to St. Thomas with her and promised I would return that same day. She was relentless, saying that I had worked too hard for my high school diploma not to attend my graduation. I remember her saying that despite all the obstacles and trials that came my way, I endured and persevered.

With no other choice, I left for St. Thomas to attend my graduation because of my respect and admiration for my daughter's grandmother. The day after my high school graduation, I went to return to Puerto Rico. My daughter stayed in Puerto Rico for four months, and I never left her side again.

Upon my daughter's release from the hospital, she and I returned to St. Thomas. With the help of my daughter's grandmother for the first six months, all my daughter's needs, and mine, were taken care of. However, things would eventually change because I knew I needed to start supplying all my daughter's needs and care for us both. Trying to find daycare services for my daughter so I could obtain full-time employment wasn't easy. My daughter's grandmother came to the rescue once again by asking her cousin to give me a job as the secretary of his concrete trucking business. He agreed that I could work in his office while Abigail lays in the playpen beside my desk. This opportunity was heaven-sent. But after a while, I struggled to support my daughter and myself. I had decided to give birth to my daughter, and she was my responsibility. Knowing that I was the person she looked to for protection, provision, and love, I had to decide to provide, protect, and love her even when it seemed impossible.

By making this declaration over our lives, I knew I had to make necessary changes that would not be comfortable. It was time to grow up and be the mother that my child deserved. I knew I had to do more to provide and care for my daughter and myself. Things got exceedingly difficult. But I refused to give up. I remember my daughter and I were hungry and homeless on the island of St. Thomas, where my family resided. However, God always sent the right people at the right time to help me in my area of need. I will be forever grateful for all the individuals God sent to help my daughter and me with food, clothing, and a roof over our heads. I even remember picking bushes from the tree outside of my apartment and boiling it to make bush tea so my daughter could have something to eat.

I always knew something was not right with my daughter due to her level of development for her age range. She wasn't doing what normal babies would do at her age. I remember taking her to the doctor on the island of Puerto Rico every month, but no one could tell me what was wrong with her process of child development. One day, we visited one of her regular monthly doctor's appointments in Puerto Rico. The gynecologist sat in for the pediatrician, and after calling me and my daughter in, she asked, "Have you ever heard of Cerebral Palsy?"

I hadn't.

She told me that my daughter was not developing according to the typical stages of child development. Abigail was at the age where she should be holding her bottle, turning over on the bed, sitting up, crawling, and trying to walk. I will never forget the doctor's words: "I have a very strong inclination that your daughter has Cerebral Palsy." Although these words would stay with me forever, I took those words as my ammunition to fight as hard as possible to learn about the condition and how I could help my daughter achieve her developmental milestones despite this diagnosis.

The 3 C's in Life: Choice, Chance, and Change. You must make the choice to take the chance if you want anything in life to change.

Your Air Mask First

I grew up believing that I was destined to be able to support, inspire, motivate, encourage, and uplift others. I can remember the feelings I experienced when I aided in resolving an issue or meeting a need. The goosebumps, the smiles, and the sense of feeling appreciated were overwhelming. I lived to help others. Although helping others was a passion of mine, it truly did not make logical sense. I grew up in a very toxic environment. I had experienced pain and unimaginable treatment that no child, or anyone, should endure, especially from people who are supposed to protect them.

I will share many of these experiences and others in later chapters. However, I have experienced enough to fill up multiple books. They could culminate several lifetimes of adverse childhood and traumatic experiences for others.

I often reflect on my life and know that my faith strengthened me to endure. My faith was all I had during many unimaginable adversities that I faced. That is why one of the most perplexing things about me was my tendency to want to help others. Why was that? Was it because I needed help, and no one responded to me when I was down and out? This was a heart-piercing moment that hit home.

However, doing so opened my eyes to one of my life's most significant revelations: *I must put on my air mask first!* Anyone who has flown on a plane has heard the crew go over the safety instructions. "In a case of decompression or drop in cabin pressure, an oxygen mask will drop from the overhead area… secure your mask first, and then assist the other person…"

There is much to be said about those instructions that can transform our lives!

However, the most ironic thing about those words is the timing in which they are spoken and how they mirror situations in life. The most critical instructions on an airplane are provided when most passengers are trying to *get settled on the plane.*

Some passengers have rushed to the airport to ensure they get through the security gate on time. Others may have had a long layover. They are finally getting on the last plane home. Then others are so excited about where they are going or enjoying their conversations with friends and loved ones.

A great life lesson is missed between the hustle and bustle of coming and going!

Make sure you do not start seeing yourself through the eyes of those who don't value you.

Self-Care: The Best Care

The topic of self-care has been receiving some attention lately. There has been extensive revelation regarding the need for self-care. There have also been many things that could be improved about the application of it as well.

I often converse about the need for self-care with my family, friends, and others. The various perspectives taken about their definition of self-care and how they carry it out are always interesting. Everyone has their spin on what self-care means. And that is truly okay.

However, most people have limited knowledge about self-care, often defining it more in superficial than practical terms. The prevailing picture and definition of self-care that most people provide, especially women, are something to the effect of mani-pedis and sipping mimosas, while overlooking beautiful scenery on vacation.

Yes, pampering and vacations are great forms of self-care, but they are not the only, nor the best form of self-care. Limiting self-care to those forms puts people who need it at a disadvantage. Think about it. How often do we take vacations? How many people have disposable income to do these types of things regularly?

Self-care should be free of expensive recreation or periodic events and outings. Self-care should occur daily in our lives.

If we consider self-care to be like the examples previously mentioned, many of us will set ourselves up for failure because self-care will become unattainable or have limited access for most individuals. Waiting for a yearly vacation or once-a-month pampering to practice self-care can put us in a dysfunctional state of mind.

Thus, self-care should occur continuously through small tasks, rituals, and routines that promote our mental, physical, and spiritual well-being. This is like maintenance to us that avoids more extensive breakdowns and issues in the future.

To position self-care in a multifaceted perspective, think of the various aspects that self-care touches. Self-care is holistic in nature. We are multi-part beings filled with thoughts and feelings, live in a physical body, and want a sense of purpose.

Therefore, we must strengthen and supply maintenance to our mind, body, soul, and spirit.

I do not know why we all hang on to something we are better off letting go.

Guard Your Mental Space

Protecting our mental space is one of the most vital forms of self-care. Our mind is a machine that can produce, reproduce, and inspire. However, it also can limit and discourage as well.

How we use our minds decides how we view life, how we make choices, and what we consciously allow in our lives.

What are you doing to protect your mind?

Do you allow your thoughts to wander?

Are you allowing people and things to contaminate your mental space?

Protecting your thoughts, desires, and your identity will keep you focused. Your thoughts are immensely powerful and can lead you down productive paths or dangerous circumstances.

Though a lot can be said about the mind, one of the most powerful tools to use for self-care is to set realistic expectations for yourself and others. A majority of people's issues stem from having unrealistic expectations.

As much as we may not like to hear it, not everyone will live in a magical environment where everything is harmonious. People will inevitably let you down, offend you, or cannot say or do things how we believe they should be done.

Furthermore, not everyone will be a millionaire; well, at least not tomorrow. There's always hope for the future. However, achieving remarkable success through innovation, creating a product, or building a brand does not come overnight. You may fail several times, go bankrupt multiple times, or even lose close family members and friends before succeeding.

I say those things because we all must find peace in knowing that life may not be ideal or even fair. Just because you have the dream job and money you've always wanted, the husband, and the children doesn't mean life will be perfect.

People will say and do inappropriate, unexpected, and hurtful things to you – both intentionally and unintentionally. Such is life. Knowing and expecting that others may not always do what we want them to do sets realistic expectations.

This allows them the space to be human and not feel as if they must be perfect, walking on eggshells around you. Releasing others enables us to open our hearts to build the foundation for genuine forgiveness when needed.

Freedom from others' expectations and construct of us is very empowering in our lives and that of others.

Feeling the need to be perfect or live up to an unrealistic expectation is highly damaging to us. Attempting to do so can put us in a bad mental space. That's why it's ideal for us to give and receive grace, knowing that no one is perfect.

In addition to creating realistic expectations, we must not allow our thoughts to wander and run wild. Never dwell on your failures.

Don't dwell on unrealistic expectations that others place on you!

Don't set up impractical deadlines to achieve your goals! Be consistent and intentional in reaching milestones that you have set up. He who fails to plan plans to fail.

Set a time limit for yourself to think about, reflect on, and revisit a failure. There are always lessons to learn from failure and our shortcomings. Knowledge, experience, and tools can be carried forward and developed from the situation.

So, reflect and extract what can be carried forward from it. But, come to a point where you confront negative thoughts with positive affirmations about who you are despite the results. Confess proclamations about the success of your future. There is power in your I AM:

- I am more than enough.
- I am complete, whole, and happy.
- I am not the sum of what I have or what I achieve.
- I am beautiful and worthy, and I walk in an abundance of love.
- I am confident in my abilities to achieve my goals and my dream.
- I am strong and resilient.
- I am able to overcome all challenges and do so because I am courageous, resilient, and tenacious!

And because of my I AMs, I have the power to create the life and lifestyle I want, and I have all I need to be successful. I know I even *deserve* the success and the happiness that derives from it.

Life will test you.

A Vicious Cycle

For the life of me, I could not figure out why I attracted broken men, angry men, men with commitment issues, arrogant and immature men, and, of course, abusive men! It was as though I had a sign on my forehead that read, "Will salvage men and make them whole again for free!"

To my wits' end, I wanted to figure this mystery out. Was this my plight in relationships? I do believe in contributing to relationships. I also believe in reasonable sacrifices to make the relationship work. However, I didn't believe I, or anyone, should have the sole responsibility of making the relationship thrive.

Too often, one person takes on that role in a relationship. As for my relationships, I was usually the one championing the cause and the one who was trying to be helpful. I was the one who was a cheerleader to the man and a laborer to his dream. I was the one who still believed in the vision when my significant other had clocked out and decided to keep me working until he found something better.

In doing this time and time again, I knew I needed to figure out why I felt the need to help others to this degree. I had to look at myself in the mirror because I was the only common denominator in all these situations. Why do I keep sacrificing so much with little to nothing in return? It was as though I was programmed to help others. I struggled to determine why and how I would continually fall into the same trap.

Be strong and courageous. Do not be afraid, for the Lord, your God will be with you wherever you go.

Beyond Being Strong

I honestly believe one of the things that's often taken out of context and misapplied is being strong. How often can you recall telling someone or being told, "Just be strong. Everything will be all right!"

When combined, the two parts of that phrase create a strong myth about how life and situations work. Your ability to *be strong* in situations doesn't automatically mean that the situation will work out in your favor or to your liking. Conversely, because a situation doesn't turn out how you believed it should have does not mean you were weak.

Often, we are caught up in a strength paradox and forget two powerful tools in navigating life and relationships: wisdom and courage. You need the wisdom to acknowledge, accept, and view situations objectively and the courage to call the situation for what it is and walk away from harm.

I say that not because it's easy—but because it is necessary!

We should never confuse being strong with the need to endure abuse, domestic violence, and trauma. We must understand that exposing ourselves to these behaviors and circumstances has long-term, residual effects on us! Those effects are seen far beyond the traumatic events and toxic relationships.

Therefore, you must be the master and steward of your environment. It's okay to limit access to you. There's nothing wrong with expressing conditions for your presence and participation in relationships. It's prudent to be in relationships with *healthy* conditions.

What do I mean about healthy conditions?

Healthy conditions in relationships are called *norms* and *boundaries*.

> You must fight through some bad days to earn the best days of your life.

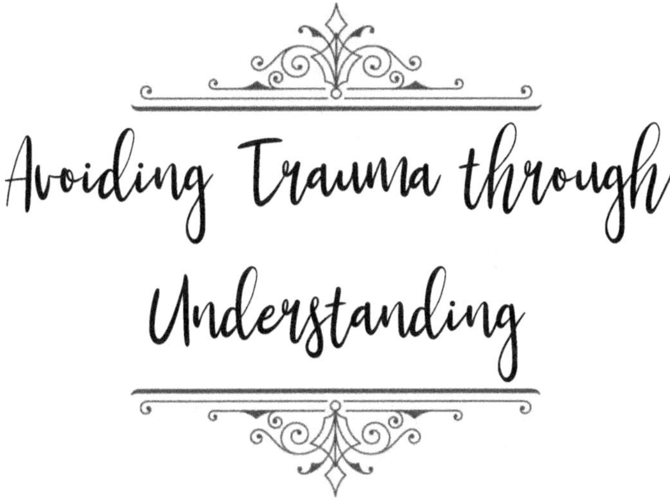

Avoiding Trauma through Understanding

Norms in relationships can be tricky sometimes. This is where communication is critical. You must realize and be committed to the paradigm of thought that everyone is raised differently. We have been in different relationships and have had different expectations asked of us. So, your normal may differ from their normal, and vice versa.

Thus, it is healthy to communicate needs, a.k.a. *norms*, in your relationship. *Norms* can include supporting one another at events, spending holidays with family, incorporating certain traditions, and consulting before making certain decisions (i.e., lending money over specific amounts, taking extended time away, etc.).

Conversely, expressing your expected needs and norms related to specific desires and functions in your relationship is essential. Otherwise, you and your partner could be miles apart from your expectations in vital areas of your relationship. For example, your norm about sex maybe every day. Your significant other's norm could be once a month.

You may have been in relationships where people have been romantic and lavished you with expensive gifts. Your new partner may be geared differently than that. They may not automatically be romantic or think of ways to spend time with you.

But if you express that those things are important, your partner may do their due diligence to schedule a time to do things that are meaningful to you. They can't fix or change what they don't know that you expect. Keep this in mind as well; though your partner may meet you where you are or in the middle ground in some areas, you may have to adjust your expectations in others.

So having conversations around expectations can be essential to your relationship. Doing so can prevent unnecessary friction and discord between you and your partner. Setting a foundation of understanding could help reduce and sometimes end trauma in relationships.

Reasonable boundaries are essential as well. Some people make the two concepts identical, but they are distinct. Norms correlate to how the relationship will function. Boundaries deal with what behaviors are acceptable and unacceptable in the relationship.

Healthy boundaries are necessary for any relationship. Two critical boundaries to set are physical as well as emotional. Both boundaries play an essential role in a healthy relationship. When levied through communication and honored through commitment, relationships can flourish.

Physical boundaries are more objective and easily noticed when violated. When someone hits you, slaps you, or pushes you down, it is clear that boundaries have been crossed. However, emotional boundaries are just as important. When a person constantly manipulates, controls, or dictates how you feel about yourself and see the world, you will find yourself in a highly volatile state.

Never forget how rare you are.

Each boundary protects a part of your holistic well-being. More importantly, they can prove relationship deal breakers and the relationship termination point. Having proven expectations in both areas set the possibility of consequences if violated. Mainly, the relationship will end. The consequences should not be that someone will be punched in the face or cursed out.

Understanding, developing, and honoring norms and boundaries can help strengthen relationships and aid in avoiding trauma. They also supply a threshold of what is acceptable or unacceptable in a relationship. They lay out an anticipation of what to expect and not to expect in the relationship.

Healthy relationships are built on communicating and setting up norms and boundaries.

Never make the mistake of automatically expecting your new relationship to work or to have elements from your earlier relationships. Your new partner does not know the norms you had in the past. Don't fall into the trap of believing this person is perfect for you. Just because the person is what you've always dreamed of doesn't mean they will automatically know the intricacies of what you expect, wish, or want in a relationship.

You must communicate what you want and expect!

You also must communicate what you do not want and will not accept!

People cannot meet your expectations or change if they do not know the standards they are being held to in relationships.

Rolling the eyes, getting angry, shutting down, being frustrated, yelling, or pulling away does not substitute for established norms and boundaries. The expected norms and boundaries must be clear-cut and defined if there is to be a foundation for relationships to start and grow. Nothing should be left to chance.

Know who you are.

ANTHOLOGIES AND OTHER BOOKS

Presented by Telishia Berry

Ready to publish *your* book?

Contact us now at **www.striveipg.com** for a consultation on how we can help your publishing dreams come true!

www.ingramcontent.com/pod-product-compliance
Lightning Source LLC
Chambersburg PA
CBHW050559160726
48003CB00002B/960